Kylie Jean
DINNER
Recipe Queen

by Gail Green
and Marci Peschke

PICTURE WINDOW BOOKS
a capstone imprint

Kylie Jean is published by Picture Window Books
A Capstone Imprint
1710 Roe Crest Drive
North Mankato, Minnesota 56003
www.mycapstone.com

Copyright © 2019 by Picture Window Books

Library of Congress Cataloging-in-Publication Data
Cataloging-in-Publication information is on file with the Library of Congress.

ISBN 978-1-5158-2849-5 (library binding)
ISBN 978-1-5158-2853-2 (paperback)
ISBN 978-1-5158-2857-0 (eBook PDF)

Editor: Mari Bolte
Designer: Tracy McCabe
Production Specialist: Kris Wilfahrt

Photo Credits:
All recipe photos by Capstone Studio/Karon Dubke, except Shutterstock:
etorres, 11 (zucchini and spiral slicer)

Design elements: Shutterstock

Printed and bound in the United States of America.
PA021

TABLE OF CONTENTS

Hey y'all, I think I hear NANNY AND PA'S dinner bell clanging. It must be TIME TO EAT! These recipes are so TASTY you'll want seconds. You can impress your whole family with this book of DELICIOUS DINNER RECIPES. The best part about these is that they're fun to make and fun to eat! Try my SAUCY CHICKEN ON A STICK and say "arr!" and "mmm" with PIRATE QUEEN TUNA BOATS. Spiralize your veggies for MISS CLARABELLE'S ZOODLES, and make a double batch of homemade pizza dough for NYC VACAY PIZZA and SOFT GARLIC HERB BREADSTICKS. Get out the pots and pans, because we're going to be making a *delicious mess!*

CONVERSIONS

1/4 teaspoon	1.25 grams or milliliters
1/2 teaspoon	2.5 g or mL
1 teaspoon	5 g or mL
1 tablespoon	15 g or mL
1/4 cup	57 g (dry) or 60 mL (liquid)
1/3 cup	75 g (dry) or 80 mL (liquid)
1/2 cup	114 g (dry) or 125 mL (liquid)
2/3 cup	150 g (dry) or 160 mL (liquid)
3/4 cup	170 g (dry) or 175 mL (liquid)
1 cup	227 g (dry) or 240 mL (liquid)
1 quart	950 mL

Fahrenheit (°F)	Celsius (°C)
325°	160°
350°	180°
375°	190°
400°	200°
425°	220°
450°	230°

This recipe is a Carter family twist on Texas BBQ! Chicken on a stick means clean fingers after eating. Our neighbor Miss Clarabelle says she can always smell them cooking on the grill!

SAUCY CHICKEN ON A STICK

INGREDIENTS:

6 boneless chicken breasts
1 ½ cups ketchup
1 ½ cups water
½ cup apple cider vinegar
¼ cup olive oil
2 tablespoons sugar
1 tablespoon lime juice concentrate, or the juice from ½ fresh lime

1 ½ teaspoons Worcestershire sauce
½ teaspoon onion powder
½ teaspoon salt
½ teaspoon chili powder
¼ teaspoon garlic powder

SPECIAL TOOLS:

wooden or metal skewers

INSTRUCTIONS:

1. With an adult's help, cut the chicken breasts into 1 ½–inch (3.8–centimeter) cubes. Set aside.

2. Pour the rest of the ingredients into a saucepan. Have an adult cook the sauce over low heat for 5 to 7 minutes. Stir constantly.

3. Remove from heat and cool completely. Pour half of the sauce into a container to use as a dipping sauce. Cover and store in the refrigerator.

4. Place the chicken in a large resealable bag. Pour the remaining sauce mixture over the chicken. Stir until all the pieces are coated. Close the bag and refrigerate. Marinate for 1 to 1 ½ hours.

5. Carefully, and with an adult's help, slide 4 chicken cubes onto each skewer. Leave ½ inch (0.6 cm) between each piece. Discard the marinade.

6. Ask an adult to grill the skewers over medium—high heat for 3 minutes per side or until the chicken is no longer pink inside.

7. Pour the dipping sauce into small bowls, and serve.

CREATIVE OPTIONS:

Use boneless chicken strips instead of the cubed chicken breast. Marinate per instructions but thread the strips on the skewer like a ribbon. Adjust cooking time as needed.

For a hotter sauce, add Cayenne pepper to taste or substitute hot sauce instead of the ketchup.

Miss Clarabelle loves to garden, but she's always trying to think of ways to use up her extra veggies. I'm going to surprise her with Zoodles for her birthday!

MISS CLARABELLE'S ZOODLES

MEATBALLS:
1 cup fresh carrots and/or broccoli, washed and cut into chunks
1 pound (16 ounces) ground beef
2 eggs, beaten
½ cup bread crumbs
1 tablespoon dried minced onion
2 teaspoons garlic powder
1 teaspoon dried parsley flakes
1 teaspoon oregano
½ teaspoon basil
¼ teaspoon salt
¼ teaspoon pepper

NOODLES:
2 ½ pounds (40 ounces) fresh zucchini (4–5 medium zucchini), unpeeled
4 tablespoons cooking oil
2 teaspoons fresh garlic, minced
⅛ teaspoon red pepper flakes (optional)

TOPPING:
½ cup Parmesan cheese, grated

SPECIAL TOOLS:
blender
cooking spray
vegetable spiralizer
tongs

TIP:
If you don't have a spiralizer, use a vegetable peeler to grate long noodles from the zucchini. You can also find already-spiralized vegetables in some grocery stores.

CREATIVE OPTION:
Use your spiralizer on other veggies! Beets, carrots, butternut squash, sweet potatoes, and other hard root vegetables also make good zoodles. Spiralize apples, cucumbers, or cabbage for a fun crunch.

continued next page

INSTRUCTIONS:

1. Ask an adult to preheat oven to 350 degrees.

2. With an adult's help, puree the vegetables in the blender.

3. Mix the pureed veggies with the rest of the meatball ingredients in a medium bowl.

4. Lightly coat a baking sheet with cooking spray.

5. Shape the meat mixture into 1–inch (2.5 cm) balls. Place them on the baking sheet.

6. Bake for 30 minutes. Have an adult remove the baking sheet from the oven. Cover with tinfoil to keep warm.

7. Wash the zucchini. Ask an adult to cut off the zucchini ends.

8. With an adult's help, use the spiralizer to make long noodles with the zucchini.

9. Ask an adult to heat the oil in a large skillet over medium heat. Add garlic and pepper flakes. Stir until the oil begins to bubble.

10. With an adult's supervision, add the zucchini noodles to the skillet. Gently toss them with tongs to coat. Sauté for 5 to 6 minutes, stirring throughout the cooking process so the zoodles cook evenly.

11. Top with meatballs and grated Parmesan cheese. Serve immediately.

CREATIVE OPTION:

For a vegetarian option, replace the meat with 1 ½ to 2 cups cooked beans, such as lentils or chickpeas, or 1 ½ cups each of cauliflower and quinoa pureed together. Slowly add the bread crumbs until meatballs form. You might not need the whole amount!

Increase the oven temperature to 425 degrees, brush the meatballs with olive oil, and check them every 5 minutes. They will probably only need to cook for 15 to 20 minutes.

Daddy says cornbread and bacon are double delicious. Ugly Brother agrees! Momma has a special wooden spoon she uses just for stirring cornbread. Sometimes she even lets me help!

CORNY BACON CORNBREAD

INGREDIENTS:

2 cups cornmeal

1 cup flour

½ cup sugar

1 teaspoon baking powder

1 teaspoon baking soda

1 ½ cups buttermilk

2 eggs, beaten

1 tablespoon cooking oil

½ cup shredded cheddar cheese, or other cheese of your choice

4 strips bacon, cooked, drained, and crumbled

½ cup sweet corn kernels, cooked and drained

SPECIAL TOOLS:

9-inch (23-cm) pie pan

cooking spray

INSTRUCTIONS:

1. Ask an adult to preheat oven to 425 degrees.

2. Lightly coat the inside of the pie pan with cooking spray. Place the pan inside the oven while it preheats.

3. Combine the cornmeal, flour, sugar, baking powder, and baking soda in a mixing bowl.

4. Mix the buttermilk, eggs, and oil together in a separate bowl. Add the cheese, bacon, and corn. Pour into the dry ingredients and stir just to combine.

5. Have an adult remove the preheated pie pan from the oven. Pour the batter mixture into the pan.

6. Bake for 30 to 35 minutes or until the top is golden brown.

CREATIVE OPTION:
For a little kick, add diced jalapeño peppers.

We traveled to New York when Daddy won an award for work. I had a big ol' slice of New York-style pizza while wearing the crown momma bought me at the Statue of Liberty. We like to make this pizza when we want to remember our trip.

NYC VACAY PIZZA

DOUGH:
1 cup warm water
1 package dry yeast
1 teaspoon honey
3 tablespoons olive oil
1 teaspoon salt
3 cups flour

SAUCE:

1 teaspoon olive oil
1 pound mild Italian sausage, divided into 1-inch (2.5-cm) chunks
1 small onion, peeled and diced
14 ½-ounce (411 gram) can diced tomatoes, drained
6-ounce (170 gram) can tomato paste

TOPPING:
2 tablespoons dried oregano
2 teaspoons olive oil
pizza toppings, such as pepperoni, sliced green peppers, mushrooms, olives, onions, ground beef, ham, spinach, or diced tomatoes

32 ounces (907 grams) mozzarella cheese, shredded
½ cup Parmesan cheese, grated

SPECIAL TOOLS:
cooking spray
rolling pin

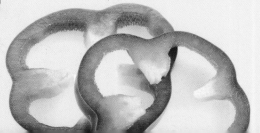

continued next page

INSTRUCTIONS:

1. Pour the warm water into a large mixing bowl. Add the yeast and honey. Stir to dissolve. Let sit for 10 to 15 minutes, or until bubbles form.

2. Add the oil, salt, and half the flour into the yeast mixture. Stir to combine.

3. Slowly add the remaining flour. Mix until you have a dough that is still moist but does not stick to your fingers.

4. Knead the dough for 6 to 7 minutes on a well—floured work surface. Place in an oiled bowl and cover. Let the dough rise in a warm place for 1 to 2 hours.

5. While the dough rises, make the sauce. Ask an adult to heat the oil in a skillet.

6. Add the sausage, and cook until browned. Remove the meat and drain well.

7. Add the diced onion to the same pan, and cook until softened. Pour in the tomatoes and tomato paste. Cook until slightly thickened. Set aside and let cool.

8. Ask an adult to preheat oven to 450 degrees.

9. Coat two baking sheets with cooking spray.

10. Once the dough has risen, split the dough ball in half. Use a rolling pin to press and shape it into two thin rectangles. Place one dough rectangle on each baking sheet.

TIPS:
The water should be just warmer than room temperature. If it is too warm, it will kill the yeast, and your dough won't rise.

Use refrigerated pizza dough or packaged crust to shorten the pizza-making process.

11. Spoon the tomato sauce evenly onto each pizza. Sprinkle the oregano and olive oil over each.

12. Scatter the cooked sausage chunks evenly over the dough. Add additional toppings, if desired.

13. Generously cover the pizzas with mozzarella and Parmesan cheese.

14. With an adult's supervision, bake for 25 to 30 minutes or until the cheese is slightly browned and bubbly. Have the adult remove the pans from the oven, and cut the slightly cooled pizza into pieces.

CREATIVE OPTIONS:

Use leftover Saucy Chicken or Zoodle meatballs for pizza toppings.

Make a double batch of dough and use the rest for Soft Garlic Herb Breadsticks.

Pizza and breadsticks go together like a suitcase and vacation.
You can't have one without the other! You can use the NYC Vacay
pizza dough to make these tasty twisted sticks.

SOFT GARLIC HERB BREADSTICKS

INGREDIENTS:

NYC Vacay Pizza Dough

3 cloves garlic, minced

1 teaspoon garlic powder

3 tablespoons fresh parsley, minced
(or 1 tablespoon dried parsley)

1 tablespoon dried basil

1 tablespoon dried oregano

2 tablespoons olive oil

¼ cup mozzarella cheese, shredded

2 tablespoons butter, melted

¼ cup Parmesan cheese, shredded

SPECIAL TOOLS:

cooking spray

rolling pin

pizza cutter

pastry brush

INSTRUCTIONS:

1. Ask an adult to preheat oven to 425 degrees. Lightly coat a baking sheet with cooking spray.

2. Divide the dough in half. Working with one piece at a time, roll dough into 6-by-10-inch (15.2-by-25.4-cm) rectangles.

3. Combine garlic, herbs, and oil in a small bowl.

4. Spread the herb mixture evenly over the dough rectangles.

5. Use a pizza cutter to slice the rectangles into 1-inch (2.5-cm)-wide strips. Carefully twist each strip and place them on the cookie sheet. Sprinkle the strips with mozzarella cheese.

6. With an adult's help, bake the breadsticks for 9 to 11 minutes or until slightly golden. Brush lightly with melted butter. Sprinkle Parmesan cheese on top.

Texas Charm hash is exactly what a rodeo queen needs before the big event!
Don't forget to add some Texas toast, too. I like mine with butter and jam.
Ugly Brother says he wants his with peanut butter!

TEXAS CHARM ROAST BEEF HASH WITH EGGS

INGREDIENTS:

2 cups pre-cooked pot roast or beef brisket

3 tablespoons oil

½ cup onion, diced

1 medium red bell pepper, seeded and diced

1 clove garlic, minced

2 large baking potatoes, peeled and diced

¼ cup beef broth

1 cup BBQ sauce

4 to 6 eggs

2 green onions, sliced

INSTRUCTIONS:

1. With an adult's help, chop, shred, or finely dice the cooked meat. Set aside.

2. Have an adult heat the oil in a large pan. Cook onions and pepper over medium heat for 3 to 4 minutes.

3. Add the garlic and potatoes. Cook another 12 to 15 minutes. Stir and flip often, until the potatoes are evenly browned.

4. Reduce heat to low. Add the shredded meat, beef broth, and BBQ sauce until warmed through.

5. Cook the eggs as preferred in a separate pan. Serve on top of the hash. Drizzle the eggs with BBQ sauce and garnish with green onions.

TIPS:

Look for precooked pot roast or brisket in the heat-and-eat meals section of your grocery store. You could also use other types of cooked meat, such as roasted chicken or pork, or smoked sausage.

Add more vegetables, such as zucchini or sweet potatoes, for a vegetarian option. Then stir in cubes of firm tofu and vegetable stock instead of the meat and beef broth.

CREATIVE OPTIONS:

Use a 32-ounce (907 gram) bag of frozen diced potatoes or hash browns instead of fresh potatoes. Or leave the potatoes out of the hash, and serve over mashed potatoes, baked potatoes, or scrambled eggs instead.

Granny is a super soup maker! Her Everything Goes Chicken Noodle Soup is famous in Jacksonville because she puts so many tasty ingredients in it. We should call it noodle surprise soup!

EVERYTHING GOES CHICKEN NOODLE SOUP

INGREDIENTS:

whole rotisserie chicken, cooked
6 cups water
1 bay leaf
¾ cup onion, diced
2 tablespoons fresh parsley, chopped
3 stalks of celery, sliced

3 carrots, peeled and sliced
1 cup green cabbage, shredded
2 cups pasta of your choice, cooked and drained

SPECIAL TOOLS:

large stock pot

INSTRUCTIONS:

1. With an adult's help, shred or chop the meat from the rotisserie chicken. Store covered in the refrigerator.

2. Place the chicken carcass, including the wing and leg bones, in the stock pot. Fill the pot with enough water to cover the bones. Add the bay leaf. With an adult's supervision, cover and simmer the stock for about 45 minutes. Remove and discard the bones and bay leaf.

3. Add onion and parsley to the stock and simmer for an additional 15 minutes.

4. Add the celery, carrots, and cabbage. Cook an additional 20 to 30 minutes, or until vegetables are tender.

5. Add the chicken and pasta to the soup. Heat on low for 3 to 4 minutes before serving.

TIPS:
You can find rotisserie chickens in the deli area of your grocery store.
You could substitute boneless, skinless chicken breasts or thighs instead too.
Ask an adult to cook them for you.

To go vegan, skip the chicken and use vegetable broth instead of water for more flavor.
Add diced silken tofu or seitan at the end. (And make sure the pasta is vegan!)

CREATIVE OPTIONS:
For a heartier soup, add canned beans, rice, and additional vegetables, such as kale,
tomatoes, or mushrooms.

Use egg noodles instead of pasta. Cook fine egg noodles in the soup for 5 to 7 minutes.

Shiver me timbers, these tuna boats are good! My friend Cara said we should make them part of our pirate code. "The ship's cook should serve Tuna boats at every meal." Good thing Ugly Brother's not the cook anymore. We'd never see a bite!

PIRATE QUEEN TUNA BOATS

INGREDIENTS:

1 loaf of Vienna or Italian bread
2 cups canned tuna
2 cups shredded cheddar cheese
1 large dill pickle, minced
1 small onion, minced
salt and pepper to taste
1/3 cup mayonnaise
baby dill pickles

SPECIAL TOOLS:

cooking spray
toothpicks

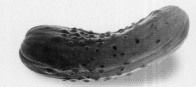

INSTRUCTIONS:

1. Ask an adult to preheat oven to 350 degrees. Position the oven rack in the upper third of the oven in broiler position.

2. Coat a baking sheet with cooking spray.

3. With an adult's help, cut the bread in half lengthwise. Place each half on the pan, cut–side–up.

4. Mix the tuna, cheese, pickle, and onion together. Stir in mayonnaise until well combined.

5. Spread the mixture onto both bread halves.

6. With an adult's supervision, cook in the oven for 15 minutes or until cheese is melted and the top begins to look golden. Ask an adult to remove the baking sheet.

7. Have an adult help slice the sandwiches into 3–inch (7.6–cm) sections. Skewer one side of a pickle with a toothpick to make a pickle flag. Stick the other end of the pickle in a sandwich section. Repeat with the rest of the pickles and toothpicks. Serve the sandwiches warm.

TIPS:
Day-old bread will hold its shape and toast better than a fresh loaf.

Cut the recipe in half and cook in a toaster oven.

CREATIVE OPTIONS:
Substitute cooked chicken, turkey, shrimp, or any cooked ground meat for the tuna.

Skip the oven and the bread and serve the tuna salad in lettuce wraps.

Football is huge in Texas, and my big brother T.J. is a Jacksonville Kings star. When it's time to tailgate, there's nothing better to bring than this caramel apple dessert salad. T.J.'s teammates say it's their favorite!

CARAMEL APPLE DESSERT SALAD

INGREDIENTS:

16—ounce (453.6 gram) can pineapple chunks and juice
2 cups mini marshmallows
½ cup sugar
1 tablespoon flour
1 ½ tablespoon white or apple cider vinegar
1 egg
1 large Granny Smith apple, unpeeled and cubed
2 large Red Delicious apples, unpeeled and cubed
1 ½ cups salted peanuts
8—ounce (226.8 gram) container whipped topping
mini chocolate chips

SPECIAL TOOLS:

whisk

INSTRUCTIONS:

1. Drain the pineapple chunks. Save the juice.

2. Combine the pineapple chunks and marshmallows in a bowl. Mix well, cover, and refrigerate for 6 to 8 hours.

3. Ask an adult to cook the pineapple juice in a saucepan over low heat. Whisk in the sugar, flour, vinegar, and egg. Cook until the mixture thickens. Cool and pour into a bowl. Cover and refrigerate 6 to 8 hours.

4. Combine the two cooled mixtures in a large mixing bowl. Stir in the apples and peanuts.

5. Fold in whipped topping. Sprinkle mini chocolate chips over the top.

It can get cold on Arrowhead Lake during the Winter Catfish Classic Fishing Contest.
Pa and I always bring Nanny's hot chocolate along to keep warm.
I think it even helped us catch Granddaddy Whiskers!

CATFISH CLASSIC COCOA

FOR THE WHIPPED CREAM:

2 cups heavy whipping cream
½ cup powdered sugar
1 teaspoon peppermint extract
red food coloring

3 ½ cups whole milk
½ cup evaporated milk
1 ½ teaspoons vanilla
crushed candy canes
chocolate and red sprinkles

FOR THE HOT COCOA:

⅓ cup water
¼ cup unsweetened cocoa powder
⅓ cup sugar
pinch of salt

SPECIAL TOOLS:

metal mixing bowl
electric mixer
piping bag and icing tip
parchment paper—lined baking sheet

INSTRUCTIONS:

1. Make the whipped cream first. Chill the metal mixing bowl and whisk attachment or beaters for 15 minutes in the freezer.

2. Pour the whipping cream into the chilled bowl. Add the sugar and peppermint extract.

3. With an adult's help, beat on low until ingredients are well mixed. Increase speed to high and beat until stiff peaks form. Fold in red food coloring until you reach a shade of pink you like.

4. Spoon the whipped cream mixture into the piping bag. Pipe small swirls of whipped cream onto the parchment—paper lined baking sheet. Freeze until solid. Store in the freezer until ready to use.

5. For the cocoa, combine water, cocoa, sugar, and salt in a sauce pan.

6. Ask an adult to cook the mixture over medium heat until it boils. Let it boil for 1 minute, stirring constantly.

7. Reduce heat to a simmer. Slowly pour in milk and evaporated milk. When the mixture simmers again, remove from the heat.

8. Stir in the vanilla. Pour the hot cocoa into mugs. Garnish with frozen whipped cream, candy canes, and sprinkles.

TIP:
Make your own red food dye. Substitute pomegranate juice or the liquid from canned or bottled beets.

CREATIVE OPTION:
If you don't have a piping bag and icing tip, you can use a plastic zip-top bag instead. Cut a corner off the bag, and squeeze small piles of whipped cream onto the parchment paper-lined baking sheet. Or you can just use a spoon to make dollops of whipped cream.

On a hot day, Ugly Brother sure does like a cool treat. These meaty puppy pops make his tail wiggle waggle with joy! He gives them two barks. Peanut butter is his favorite flavor. I wonder which version your pup will like best?

UGLY BROTHER'S PUPPY PLACE POPSICLES

CROWNS:
2 cups Greek yogurt, plain
¼ cup low–sodium bone broth, liquid concentrate
½ cup 100% pure pumpkin, canned
2 tablespoons fresh parsley, minced
½ cup blueberries, fresh or frozen

SPECIAL TOOLS:
blender
silicone molds

INSTRUCTIONS:

1. Mix yogurt and bone broth in a bowl until evenly combined.

2. Scoop ¾ of the yogurt mixture into another bowl. Add pumpkin. Mix well.

3. Scoop ½ cup of the pumpkin yogurt mixture into another bowl. Stir in parsley. Refrigerate.

4. With an adult's help, blend the blueberries until pureed. Add the blueberries to the bone broth yogurt mixture that's left. Refrigerate.

5. Spoon the pumpkin mixture into the silicone molds. Place in the freezer for 30 minutes.

6.	Remove the molds from the freezer. Add a layer of the parsley mixture to each mold. Return to the freezer for 30 minutes.

7.	Remove the molds from the freezer. Add a layer of the blueberry mixture to each mold. Return to the freezer for 3 hours or until frozen. Pop frozen treats out of the mold and store in a plastic bag for up to 2 months.

TIP:
Instead of the bone broth concentrate, mix powdered bone broth into ¼ cup water or unsweetened apple juice. Or use low-sodium beef broth.

CREATIVE OPTION:
Use shredded carrots, chopped blueberries, or dried cranberries like sprinkles to decorate the popsicles.

Replace the bone broth with peanut butter for a meat-free version.

Read More

Archer, Joe, and Caroline Craig. *Plant, Cook, Eat!: A Children's Cookbook.* Watertown, Mass.: Charlesbrige Publishing, 2018.

Huff, Lisa. *Kid Chef Bakes: The Kids Cookbook for Aspiring Bakers.* Emeryville, Calif.: Rockridge Press, 2017.

Ventura, Marne, and Marci Peschke. *Kylie Jean Party Craft Queen.* North Mankato, Minn.: Picture Window Books, 2014.

Internet Sites

Use Facthound to find Internet sites related to this book.

Visit *www.facthound.com*

Just type in 9781515828495 and go!

 Check out projects, games and lots more at
www.capstonekids.com

Books in this series: